Diminishing Mexican Immigration to the United States

AUTHORS

Carl Meacham
Michael Graybeal

A Report of the CSIS Americas Program

July 2013

50 YEARS | CHARTING OUR FUTURE

CSIS | CENTER FOR STRATEGIC & INTERNATIONAL STUDIES

ROWMAN & LITTLEFIELD PUBLISHERS, INC.
Lanham • Boulder • New York • Toronto • Plymouth, UK

About CSIS—50th Anniversary Year

For 50 years, the Center for Strategic and International Studies (CSIS) has developed solutions to the world's greatest policy challenges. As we celebrate this milestone, CSIS scholars are developing strategic insights and bipartisan policy solutions to help decisionmakers chart a course toward a better world.

CSIS is a nonprofit organization headquartered in Washington, D.C. The Center's 220 full-time staff and large network of affiliated scholars conduct research and analysis and develop policy initiatives that look into the future and anticipate change.

Founded at the height of the Cold War by David M. Abshire and Admiral Arleigh Burke, CSIS was dedicated to finding ways to sustain American prominence and prosperity as a force for good in the world. Since 1962, CSIS has become one of the world's preeminent international institutions focused on defense and security; regional stability; and transnational challenges ranging from energy and climate to global health and economic integration.

Former U.S. senator Sam Nunn has chaired the CSIS Board of Trustees since 1999. Former deputy secretary of defense John J. Hamre became the Center's president and chief executive officer in April 2000.

CSIS does not take specific policy positions; accordingly, all views expressed herein should be understood to be solely those of the author(s).

Library of Congress Cataloging-in-Publication Data
CIP information available on request.

ISBN: 978-1-4422-2495-7 (pb); 978-1-4422-2496-4 (eBook)

Center for Strategic and International Studies
1800 K Street, NW, Washington, DC 20006
202-887-0200 | www.csis.org

Rowman & Littlefield Publishers, Inc.
4501 Forbes Boulevard, Lanham, MD 20706
301-459-3366 | www.rowman.com

Contents

Acknowledgments

The authors would like to thank Stephen Johnson, CSIS Americas Program senior associate and former program director, as well as the current director for the Latin America Caribbean Division at the International Republican Institute, for his guidance and preparation of the initial draft of this report. His focus on the considerable progress the Mexican economy has made in recent years, as well as the challenges it continues to confront, helped guide further versions of the report.

The authors would also like to thank Pamela K. Starr, director of the U.S.-Mexico Network, university fellow at the University of Southern California (USC) Center on Public Diplomacy, and an associate professor of teaching in the School of International Relations and in Public Diplomacy, for her careful review of the initial draft of the report. Her editing and suggestions for the report proved invaluable in portraying the nuances of U.S.-Mexico migration.

Americas Program intern scholars Tania Miranda and Jillian Rafferty also provided valuable research assistance and editing for drafting the final version of the report. Their help proved instrumental in the report's preparation.

Diminishing Mexican Immigration to the United States

Introduction

As the debate over comprehensive immigration reform takes place in the U.S. Congress, understanding the nature of immigration to the United States has perhaps never been more relevant than it is today. At the time of this report's writing, the U.S. Senate recently completed hammering out the specifics of a reform bill that was sent to the House, where many still remain skeptical as to the bill's priorities, appropriateness, cost, and utility.

The bill, called "The Border Security, Economic Opportunity, and Immigration Modernization Act," is built around three core provisions: the extension of legal status to undocumented immigrants—and an eventual path to U.S. citizenship; the strengthening of border security; and bolstered work programs to facilitate the entry and hiring of both high- and low-skilled foreign workers. Given that its passage would impact some 11 million undocumented immigrants living illegally in the United States, it is vital to understand the context of immigration to this country. What drives migrants to leave their families to find opportunities in the United States? And, what determines the nature of migrant flows to the United States?

While it is difficult to discern all of the factors that determine migration flows, the core drivers of migration remain well known: job opportunities; a lack of job opportunities or salary parity for the same job at home; and informal networks that provide jobseekers with information on employment opportunities.[1]

Mexican migration to the United States has neatly fit this pattern for over 100 years. Since the 1940s, demand in the U.S. economy for unskilled and semiskilled workers has significantly outstripped supply, creating an opportunity to attract potential migrants. For most of this time, U.S. government policy was focused on limiting the number of visas for low-skilled migrants—keeping the number allowed to enter well below the level of demand increased migration flows of undocumented workers.

At the same time, a population boom in Mexico coupled with growing economic difficulties beginning in the 1960s prevented the country from providing sufficient employment—much

1. In one survey, most unauthorized migrants returned to Mexico said they were looking for work. See Jeffrey Passel, D'Vera Cohn, Ana Gonzalez Barrera, "Net Migration from Mexico Falls to Zero and Perhaps Less," Pew Research Hispanic Center, April 23, 2012, p. 2, http://www.pewhispanic.org/2012/04/23/net-migration-from-mexico-falls-to-zero-and-perhaps-less/.

less well-paying jobs—for the huge number of new entrants into the labor force. Migrating to the United States proved attractive for many Mexicans because of proximity, and because the border was easy to cross.

Over time, migration north generated communication networks that transmitted information about job opportunities in the United States back home.

These drivers of migration remain relevant. For many Mexicans, there is still a strong incentive to migrate to the United States in search of better-paying jobs and improved standards of living for themselves and their families. Yet several of these drivers have begun to shift.

While the U.S. economy continues to create an excess of low-skilled jobs (though this saw a large dip during the 2008 recession) and communication networks continue to transmit information about job availability, the cost of migrating has increased, and the growth of jobseekers in Mexico has begun a slow but steady decline. There is clear evidence that the slow recovery of the U.S. economy and news about the availability of jobs has ended the "net zero" moment—the period when as many migrants were leaving the United States as were entering.

Recent research suggests there is growing evidence of increased unauthorized migration, that the size of the Mexican-born population in the United States has fully recovered, and that the flow of remittances to the south is bouncing back.[2] Nonetheless, the supply of Mexican workers willing to migrate appears to be on the brink of a significant decline. This is partially due to the increased cost of migrating created by changes in U.S. policy and the role of organized crime in human trafficking. But it also reflects profound demographic and economic changes in Mexico that combined can be expected to cut the supply of Mexican workers in the not-too-distant future.

As the supply of low-skilled Mexican workers declines—and if U.S. immigration policy does not provide the necessary number of visas for low-skilled workers to meet labor market demands—a change of the flow of migrants across the U.S. southern border is more likely.

While the majority of migrants to the United States have been Mexican, the demographics of migrants will shift, becoming majority Central American. This new migration dynamic will inevitably change the nature of migration policy, as it will no longer be a binational issue. No longer will Mexico be a key factor of this issue; instead, Mexico could prove an important potential partner in developing policy solutions.

---

2. Roberto Suro and Rene Zenteno, "Overview: Mexican Migration Beyond the Downturn and Deportations," *Mexican Migration Monitor* (October 2012), http://www.migrationmonitor.com/1-article/.

Reasons to Leave Mexico

Highway sign south of San Diego, California. Credit: Jonathan McIntosh. Source: FLICKR, Creative Commons, http://www.flickr.com/photos/jonathanmcintosh/4059183926/in/set-72157622469119022.]

The motivation to migrate derives from a wide range of factors but is dominated by the search for better economic opportunities abroad. This core driver is aided by the access to information about job availability and by the relative ease of migrating.

ECONOMIC GROWING PAINS

The first significant wave of Mexican migration to the United States began during the Mexican Revolution (1910–1917). The violence of the revolution pushed many Mexicans north of the border in search of safety. The impact of the revolution was the elimination of debt peonage, which had tied agricultural workers to the land for generations. As a result, for the first time in Mexican history, the country possessed an agricultural labor force that was free to move anywhere to find a new job. This new supply of Mexican workers coupled with the boom in the U.S. economy during the 1920s produced a significant migration to the United States. But with the onset of the Great Depression in the 1930s, the flow slowed; in addition, many Mexicans who had been working in the United States were deported.

World War II created a renewed demand for Mexican labor from the United States. With a large percentage of the working-age male population occupied as soldiers, the two countries agreed to create and manage the "Bracero" Program, which created a legal mechanism for the United States to import low-skilled Mexican workers. Following the war, many U.S. veterans from rural areas returned to live in cities while others took advantage of the GI Bill of Rights to obtain a university degree. As a consequence, the U.S. demand for Mexican labor continued for a generation after the war. In 1964, the United States terminated the Bracero Program to channel the U.S. demand for Mexican labor. But the program was terminated without eliminating the country's economic need for the workers covered by it or making an effort to prevent these workers from continuing to cross the border. As a consequence, what had been a legal flow of workers was transformed into an illegal flow.

Beginning in the 1970s, however, things began to change. Shifts in the U.S. economy increased demand for low-skilled workers just as more of these workers became available in Mexico. The increase in supply had much to do with problems associated with Mexico's Import Substitution Industrialization model of economic development. After generating impressive growth rates for nearly three decades, this development model became exhausted by the 1970s.

BARRIERS TO EMPLOYMENT

Various internal factors seemed to constrain job opportunities as Mexico's youth bulge came of working age. Among them were a noncompetitive commercial environment, an outdated agricultural model, and an education system more concerned with protecting its educator workforce than developing the nation's human capital.

Figure 1. Mexico—Poverty Rate

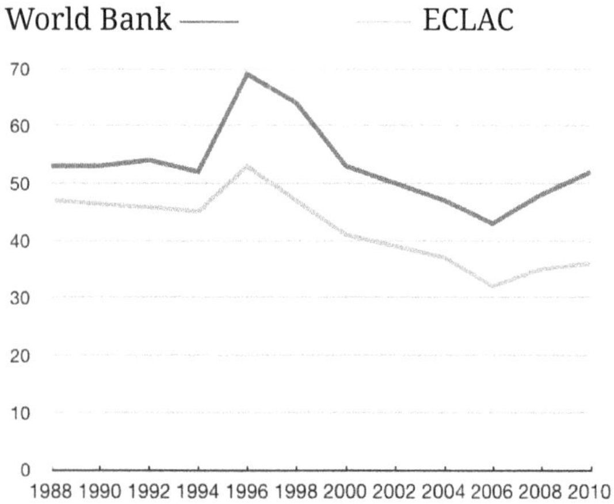

Sources: World Development Indicators, The World Bank, updated January 17, 2013; CEPALSTAT, Databases and Statistical Publications, Economic Commission for Latin America and the Caribbean.

Figure 2. Mexico—Population Growth and Total Population Growth Rate

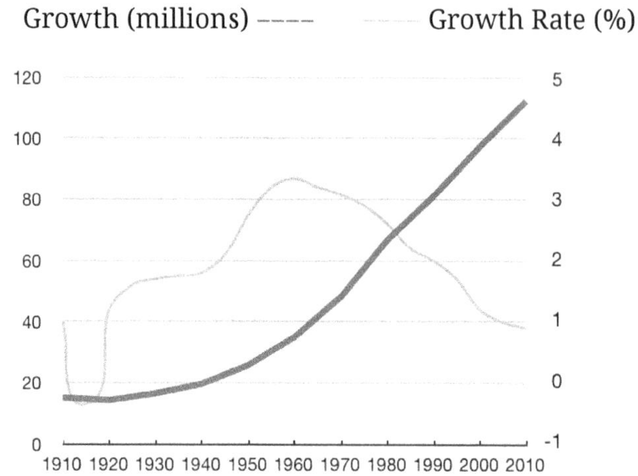

Sources: Population – National Institute of Statistics and Geography (INEGI), updated July 11, 2012. Population Growth Rate – Virgilio Partida, citing CONAPO (2002), "Demographic transition, demographic bonus and ageing in Mexico," United Nations Expert Group Meeting on Social and Economic Implications of Changing Population Age Structures, Mexico City, August 31-September 2, 2005 at http://www.un.org/esa/population/meetings/EGMPopAge/Partida_Figures.pdf.

Until the North American Free Trade Agreement (NAFTA) was implemented in 1994, the Mexican government provided subsidies and tariff protections intended to grow native businesses but in time came to prop up bloated companies offering poor services. Excess government spending, through the provision of public-sector employment and the creation and purchase of state-run firms, generated large budget deficits. The national oil company, Pemex, sustained the federal budget, which became the principal economic instrument through spending. When oil prices went up, spending rose. When prices collapsed, they suffered and debt became unsustainable.[3] Only after NAFTA did a more modern economy flourish that favored manufacturing and exports, although it still had to compete with oligopolies from the past.

Until the early 2000s, one-third or more of Mexico's population lived in rural areas. Although during the boom years from 1940 to 1970 Mexican farmers were sufficiently productive to feed the growing urban populations and industries, their productivity began to wane as the government persistently favored investments away from rural areas, toward the industrial sector and urban job creation.

In addition to the problems plaguing the agricultural sector, Mexico's public education has been swamped with a number of structural problems of its own. Compulsory education was only extended past the sixth grade in 1992.[4] While enrollments have continued to increase, corresponding to the growing population, the system has coped by creating split shifts in many schools, and by trying to expand distance learning to a technology-starved countryside.

3. Timothy J. Kehoe and Felipe Meza, "Catch-up Growth Followed by Stagnation: Mexico, 1950–2010," Working Paper 693, Federal Reserve Bank of Minneapolis, revised November 2012, pp. 14–16, http://www.minneapolisfed.org/research/wp/wp693.pdf.

4. Tim L. Merrill and Ramón Miró, eds., *Mexico: A Country Study* (Washington, DC: Library of Congress, 1996).

Likewise, the powerful teachers' union has, until very recently, controlled teacher hiring, resisted educator evaluations, and influenced budgetary decisions at the national level, hampering the system's improvement. Even given these deeply rooted problems in the Mexican education system, however, before the twentieth century, the country's economy could not provide high-skilled jobs for the graduates of the public education system. It was not until then that a shortage of human capital began contributing to the excess supply of Mexican labor.

DEMOGRAPHIC PRESSURE

The early twentieth century saw minimal (and at times even negative) population growth in Mexico. Following the Second World War, however, annual Mexican population growth took off, peaking at 3 percent in the 1960s. This rapid growth brought with it a "youth bulge"—or the swelling of the juvenile population.[5] The persistent, dramatic growth of the available labor force exerted constant pressure on the Mexican economy to create more jobs—a tall order, even in times of robust growth. Even at those moments when the economy enjoyed strong growth, it time and again proved unable to provide sufficient jobs to employ the ever-expanding labor force. And when one million or more youths joined the labor force each year with only a fraction of that many jobs available, low-skilled jobs in the United States became increasingly appealing.

DRAWN TO THE UNITED STATES

Mexico's enormous labor surplus would mean little without jobs available in the United States. Without the potential to secure employment, there is little incentive to migrate—as evidenced by the significant slowdown of migration during the Great Depression. Demographer Jeffrey Passel of the Pew Hispanic Center has noted the striking correlation between the inflow of Mexican migrants and the U.S. employment rate (Figure 3).

Figure 3. Mexican Migrant In-flow versus U.S. Employment Rate

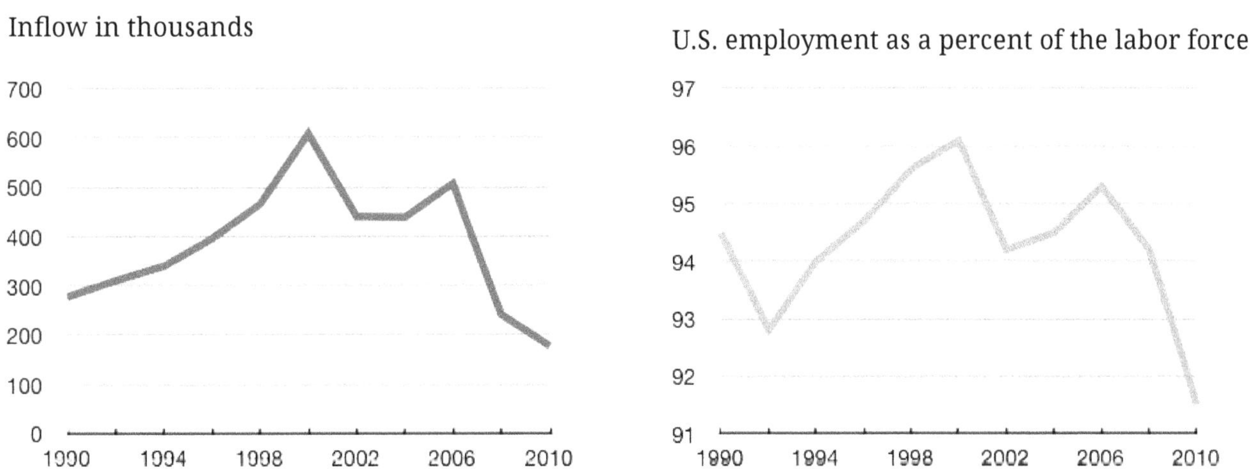

Sources: Jeffrey S. Passel, "Dealing with the Causes: Mexico's Economic Policy and Migration," Presentation at the Center for Strategic and International Studies, Washington, DC, January 11, 2011; U.S. Unemployment Rate, 1990-2010, Bureau of Labor Statistics, U.S. Department of Labor, at http://data.bls.gov/pdq/SurveyOutputServlet.

5. UN Children's Fund, "At a Glance: Mexico," http://www.unicef.org/infobycountry/mexico_statistics.html.

During the economic boom the United States enjoyed in the 1990s, some 300,000 Mexican migrants entered the country each year; the rate of inflow finally peaked at 600,000 in 2000. After the terrorist attacks on the United States in 2001 and the shallow recession that followed, migration dipped, and then picked up again as the U.S. economy and employment rate recovered. Beginning in 2006, the numbers dropped sharply and have since continued to decline.

Accordingly, the population of unauthorized Mexican migrants living in the United States rose steadily from 4.6 million in 2000 to 7.0 million in 2007, and experienced a slight decline to 6.5 million in 2010. Their desire to leave their country due to an adverse economic environment aside, Mexican immigration to the United States is driven principally by demand for labor in the latter; without good jobs available in the United States, migration stalls. And when facing fewer job opportunities at home, the migrant flow is enabled by informal networks of immigrants within the United States.

Reasons to Come to the United States

Modern patterns of Mexican migration to the United States have their roots in the traditional movements both of families across the southwestern border through California, the Rocky Mountains, and the western Great Plains, as well as of laborers who sought work on railroads and cattle ranches. But with reform of U.S. immigration policy immediately following the Bracero program, including, for example, the Immigration and Nationality Act of 1965,[6] immigration took on a new focus.

The new policy stressed quotas and prioritized keeping families together rather than setting up (or maintaining) a flexible system to manage the entry and exit of migrant workers—even though the U.S. demand for manual labor remained high. The adoption of the Immigration Reform and Control Act of 1986,[7] which provided amnesty for illegal immigrants already in the country but more strictly punished employers for knowingly hiring undocumented individuals, sought to stymie the inward flow of Mexican migrants.

Ultimately, however, the Act served more to end the circular cycle of migration than it did to end it entirely, as the more secure border incentivized migrants to stay in the United States. All in all, post-Bracero immigration policy did little to reduce the influx of migrants, driven as they were by the economic and social conditions outlined in the previous section.

The end of the twentieth century brought the introduction of the Immigration Act of 1990 and the USA Patriot Act of 2001,[8] and the implementation of limits on legal migration, capping unskilled temporary worker visas and increasing detentions of unauthorized entrants.

But even these measures did not deter undocumented job seekers from entering the country. As the U.S. economy rapidly expanded, the demand for labor grew still larger. As

6. Public Law 89–236.
7. Public Law 99–603, known as Simpson-Mazzoli after Senate sponsors Alan K. Simpson of Wyoming and Romano L. Mazzoli of Kentucky.
8. Public Laws 101–649 and 107–56.

a result, many opted to head north. Of those that sought unauthorized entry into the United States, 95 percent made it, even given increased border patrol. And once the migrants were in the country, the tortuous exit and reentry path combined with the prospect that Congress might again grant immigrants amnesty likely prompted them to stay.

This pattern remained strong until the U.S. demand for labor fell as the economy slipped into deep recession in 2008. Nearly five years later, the economy continues to stagnate. The annual growth rate is still below 2 percent, and unemployment, though now trending downward, is still above 7 percent—high for normal standards.

As domestic unemployment rose and fewer jobs—even in manual labor—were available for migrants when the recession hit, migration flows dropped correspondingly. For the first time, the Mexican-born population living in the United States declined from a peak of 12.6 million to 12 million.[9] The 80 percent of migrants who had traditionally worked low-paying jobs in the construction, transportation, and services sectors faced tougher economic straits than they had in the past.[10] As the construction industry contracted, many found themselves out of work.[11] When the cost of living in the United States remained much higher than in Mexico even during the recession, migrants increasingly preferred returning to the now more stable Mexican economy rather than continuing to reside illegally in the economically troubled United States.

Even at moments when the U.S. economy suffers through rough patches, wage disparity still contributes to Mexican immigrants' desire to stay in the United States. Though many would prefer to return to Mexico—to their families and culture—there remains a large wage gap between Mexico and its northern neighbor, whereby workers earn higher wages in the United States for the same labor. In 2009, for instance, the wage gap between Mexico's nominal manufacturing hourly wage and the equalized wage in the United States was 77 percent.[12] For this reason, once immigrants secure a job on the U.S. side of the border, it's less attractive for them to return to their country of origin—even if they are able to find a similar job at home.

Reasons to Stay in Mexico

While decreasing U.S. demand for labor has certainly contributed to the slowed inflows of Mexican migrants, so, too, have substantial changes within Mexico. Gradual adoption of structural reforms, improved competitiveness in the global economy, and more favorable domestic demographics have together slowed the growth of the Mexican labor supply even as they have sped up the growth of the economy—and, concurrently, of the country's middle class. And as Mexico continues along this trajectory, its role as a supplier of low-skilled labor

9. Passel et al., "Net Migration from Mexico Falls to Zero and Perhaps Less," p. 11.

10. See "Figure 7: Industry of Employment, by Nativity and Sex, 2009" in Kate Brick, A.E. Challinor, and Marc Rosenblum, "Mexican and Central American Immigrants in the United States" (Washington, DC: Migration Policy Institute, June 2011), p. 11, http://www.migrationpolicy.org/pubs/mexcentamimmigrants.pdf.

11. Ibid., p. 12.

12. The wage gap between nominal and equalized wages are converted in terms of purchasing power parities, and expressed in percentages. Jus Semper Global Alliance, "Wage Gap Charts: Manufacturing production-line wages," December 2011, http://www.jussemper.org/Resources/Labour%20Resources/WGC/Resources/Wage%20gap%20charts.pdf.

Figure 4. U.S. Apprehensions of Unauthorized Migrants: 2000-2011

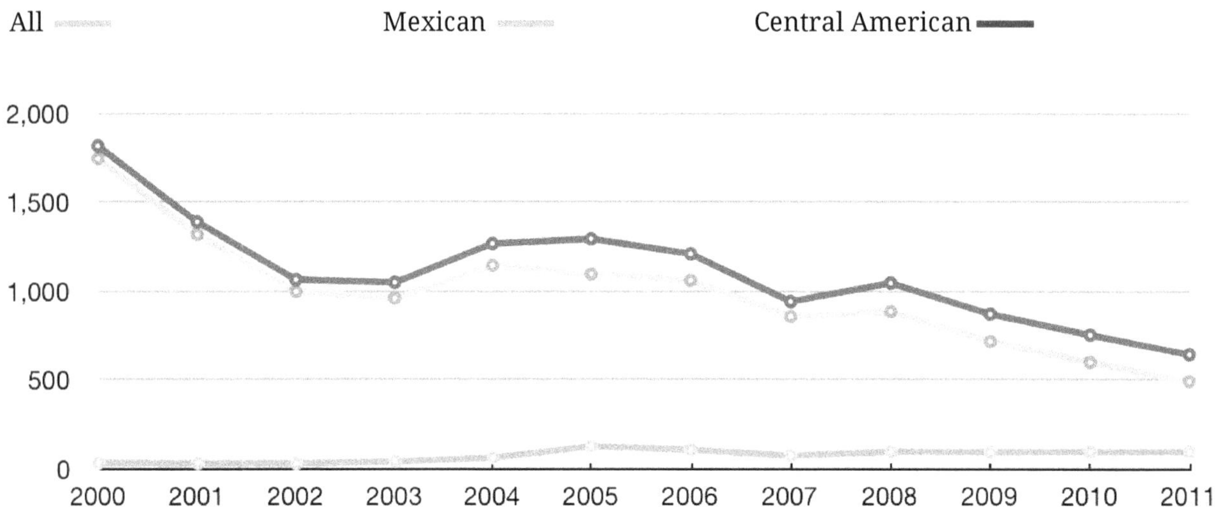

Sources: *Yearbook of Immigration Statistics,* (2000-2011) Immigration Statistics, U.S. Department of Homeland Security, http://www.dhs.gov/immigration-statistics.

to the United States will likely continue to decline.

REFORM IN MEXICO

In the 1970s, as the statist policies that guided Mexico's development over the previous two decades came under fire, the Mexican government embarked on what would be gradual but persistent economic reform, seeking to better accommodate a growing population and desires for increased political and economic freedom. Though that effort has suffered some significant setbacks over its 40-year history, Mexico has remained on the reformist path. In so doing, it has slowly but surely secured economic payoffs, including the development of cutting-edge technology in the context of an increasingly competitive economy whose solid growth rate currently exceeds Brazil's.

The reform began as the Mexican population challenged the authoritarian character of the ruling Institutional Revolutionary Party (PRI). Following disastrous *peso* devaluation in 1982, business leaders joined the push for change, demanding neoliberal economic reforms.[13] And after another financial crisis in the late 1980s, President Carlos Salinas de Gortari initiated policies designed to open Mexico's economy in what would eventually grow into the North American Free Trade Agreement (NAFTA).[14]

Though the Mexican economy suffered through further financial crisis due to a severe capital flight and devaluation in 1995, the better management of the country's fiscal policy enabled it to bounce back more quickly than in the past. Simultaneously, NAFTA bolstered

13. See Francisco E. González, *Dual Transitions from Authoritarian Rule: Institutionalized Regimes in Chile and Mexico, 1970–2000* (Baltimore, MD: Johns Hopkins University Press, 2008), pp. 79–83.

14. Trade between the two countries more than doubled between 1994 and 2003. U.S. exports to Mexico expanded by 91 percent and Mexican exports to the United States rose by 179 percent. See J.F. Nornbeck, "NAFTA at Ten: Lessons from Recent Studies," Congressional Research Service, February 13, 2004, p. 2, http://fpc.state.gov/documents/organization/34486.pdf.

trade with the United States—a commercial tie that proved pivotal for strengthening the Mexican economy. Amidst this sweeping economic reform, President Ernesto Zedillo laid plans for the country's first free and fair general elections, ending 71 years of one-party rule.

While political and economic reform had already come a long way from just 30 years before, President Vincente Fox, the National Action Party (PAN) candidate inaugurated in 2000, faced the tough reality that the government would be far from able to generate enough jobs for the large young population entering the workforce. In an attempt to mitigate this imminent problem and expand cooperation with the United States, Fox proposed a set of agreements with the northern ally that would have allowed for the free movement of labor between the two countries.

Far-reaching as this reform would have been, the U.S. government had more pressing concerns, as Fox's proposal was finalized just days before the terrorist attacks of September 11, 2001. And although border cooperation between the two governments increased, it was primarily concerned with tightening security, sharing counterterrorism intelligence, and combating drug trafficking—not with providing a legal avenue for the Mexican labor to fill the U.S. labor shortage.

Though Fox's efforts to reform U.S. immigration policy fell flat, his administration successfully worked to strengthen the Mexican economy. Under his leadership, Mexico stabilized the *peso*, reduced inflation to single digits, cut foreign debt, and invested in social programs. The country also bolstered its health care system and boosted educational achievement through increased funding for schools.[15] Both economic and political reforms surged forward throughout his presidency, keeping Mexico on a trajectory toward growth and stability.

Fox's successor, Felipe Calderón, came up against escalating violence between rival drug-trafficking gangs and the government—violence for which his administration is most remembered. Even during this turbulent period, however, Calderón pushed forward extensive economic reforms, including the elimination of some 16,000 federal rules or regulations affecting commerce, the reduction of tariffs, and the first major restructuring of Mexico's labor code since its enactment in 1931.[16] Calderón's labor reform streamlined the hiring and termination of workers, allowed for new-hire trial and training periods, better protected against discrimination, provided for hourly wages, and ended the "closed shop" (or union membership) requirement.[17] In short, despite the drug-violence challenges that plagued his administration, Calderón pushed economic and political reform further forward.

---

15. Carlos Luken, "Mexico continues to advance under Vicente Fox," Mexidata Info, September 26, 2005, http://mexidata.info/id619.html.

16. "Looking back on the Calderón years," *The Economist*, November 22, 2012, http://www.economist.com/blogs/americasview/2012/11/felipe-calderón-his-presidency-mexico?zid=309&ah=80dcf288b8561b012f603b9fd9577f0e.

17. See Stephen Johnson, "Mexican Labor Reforms—What Do They Mean," *CSIS Hemisphere Focus*, December 17, 2012, http://csis.org/publication/mexican-labor-reforms-what-do-they-mean.

TODAY: A MORE GLOBALLY COMPETITIVE MEXICO

Mexican workers; credit CIMMYT, FLICKR, Creative Commons, at http://www.flickr.com/photos/cimmyt/7798631622.

Compared to global and U.S. economic prospects, Mexico's potential now looks favorable. Following the 2009 recession, the economy rebounded with 5.5 percent growth in 2010—and although growth slowed in 2011, it stabilized between 3 and 4 percent. That growth is expected to continue, with projected growth for 2013 estimated at 3.3 percent.[18]

More notably, Mexico seems to be gaining a competitive edge in manufacturing. For much of the past decade, China's manufactured goods ate into Mexican exports to the United States. Now, as wages grow in China, labor costs there have begun to approach those of Mexico's. And when factoring in transportation costs, Mexico's proximity to the United States has helped it regain its competitive edge. While stagnant wage growth in Mexico may not be a boon for its workers, it has helped many Mexican export sectors, especially in the automotive and electronics industries, where it has boosted new job creation. Those industries have also benefited from foreign investment. One Japanese car manufacturer recently shifted its low-cost car production to Mexico, making Mexico the fourth-largest car manufacturer in the world. And flat-panel televisions are now being assembled in Juárez, even as a wireless headset manufacturer closed its plant in China and announced a US$30 million investment in Mexico last year.

Current President Enrique Peña Nieto was inaugurated amidst this manufacturing boom and Mexican economic growth. He signaled his intention to continue along Mexico's trajectory of reform early on; the day after his inauguration, he released the *Pacto por* México, a document articulating his promises to cooperate on 95 reform themes. Showcasing a new spirit of political cooperation, he coaxed the leaders of all three of Mexico's major parties to sign on. Ten days later, he sent a package of education measures to the congress that would strip the powerful educators' union of its influence over teacher hires and school budgets. And in February 2013, the government underscored the point by arresting Elba Esther Gordillo, leader of the 1.4 million strong teachers' union, on suspicion of embezzling some US$200 million in funds for her personal use.[19] In a recent development, Peña Nieto and the Mexican Congress signed a reform opening Mexico's telecommunications sector to competition, and further changes that would permit foreign investment in Pemex, the state petroleum monopoly, are anticipated later this year.

Among other plans designed to turn Mexico into one of the world's most promising markets, Peña Nieto has promised to enact tax reforms, develop an aggressive trade strategy to

18. "Mexico's economy will grow 3.3 pct in 2013, OECD says," Fox News Latino, November 27, 2012, http://latino.foxnews.com/latino/news/2012/11/27/mexico-economy-will-grow-33-pct-in-2013-oecd-says.

19. Randal C. Archibold and Elizabeth Malkin, "Powerful Mexican Teachers' Leader Accused of Embezzlement," *New York Times*, February 27, 2013, http://www.nytimes.com/2013/02/28/world/americas/elba-esther-gordillo-mexican-teachers-leader-accused-of-embezzlement.html?_r=0.

better compete with China, and push for Mexico's accession to the Trans-Pacific Partnership (TPP) trade agreement of Pacific Rim nations.[20]

CHANGING DEMOGRAPHICS

As Mexico's economic prospects continue to brighten, its shifting demographics present a more modest, but certainly hopeful, future—one that may well have profound effects on the flows of Mexican migrants to the United States. On one hand, Mexico's population growth rate, which reached upwards of 3 percent in the 1960s, has steadily declined—and, according to World Bank statistics, it was just 1.2 percent in 2011. That slowed rate alone, and the declining youth bulge associated with it, should translate into a significantly decreased pressure on new workforce entrants to migrate elsewhere.

Figure 5. Mexico–Population Growth Rate

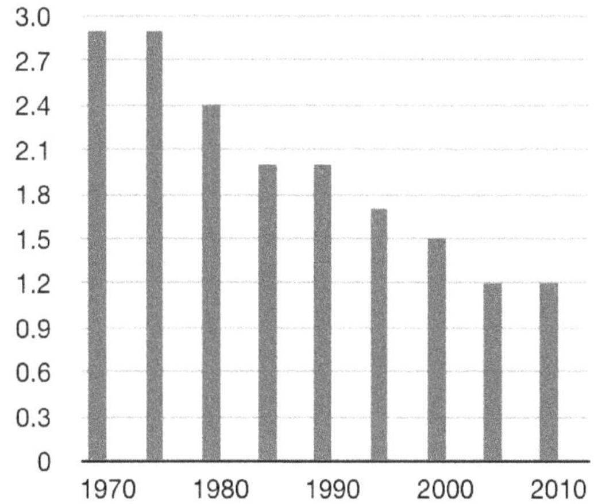

Source: "Mexico," *Data,* The World Bank, http://data.worldbank.org/country/mexico.

On the other hand, the changing population growth rate implies that the average age of Mexico's populace will advance as time passes—a reality that will test public health and social support networks, likely within as little as 20 years. Moreover, Mexico will need a younger, better educated workforce to maintain its own productivity. And high poverty rates, particularly in rural areas, are not to be ignored.[21] Nonetheless, the Mexican government's recent investments in education, the economy's robust growth, and the demographic changes generated by slowing population growth rates will likely combine to put less pressure on Mexicans to move northward, decreasing their migration to the United States.

EVOLVING CITIZEN SECURITY AND THE RULE OF LAW

Despite common misconceptions, personal security has not proven to be a major factor in sending Mexican migrants north. Though violence related to drug trafficking began to escalate in 2007, northward migration flows were—and remained—on the decline. There have, certainly, been substantial and frequent shifts in the Mexican government's attempts to curtail drug trafficking and the violent conflict associated with it. And while the success of those efforts may well be relevant to the country's ability to attract foreign investment and expand employment, citizen security itself has played little to no role in determining the cross-border

---

20. The Trans-Pacific Partnership is a proposal for an expanded version of a trade agreement that now includes Brunei, Chile, New Zealand, and Singapore. The proposed pact would add Canada, Malaysia, Mexico, Peru, the United States, Japan, and Vietnam.

21. See World Bank, "Mexico," http://data.worldbank.org/country/mexico. Also, "Mexico: National Socio-Demographic Profile," CEPALSTAT, Databases and Statistical Publications, Economic Commission for Latin America and the Caribbean (ECLAC), United Nations, http://interwp.cepal.org/cepalstat/WEB_cepalstat/Perfil_nacional_social.asp?Pais=MEX&idioma=i.

flows of Mexican migrants. As such, there is no reason to expect the ongoing conflict to obviate the downward trajectory of the Mexican supply of migrant labor.

The Changing Nature of Migration

Mexico's poor and undereducated have not been the only ones looking for work in their native country. Migrants from bordering Central American states compete as well, although the numbers probably add up to less than a half of 1 percent of the overall population. Notably, the country's international migrant stock doubled from 1980 to 1990. Contributing to the rise were refugee inflows as Central American countries endured the effects of civil conflict.

Overall migrant stock decreased when peace accords were struck. As violent crime waves began to overwhelm El Salvador, Guatemala, and Honduras in the late 1990s, migration picked up again. Some Central Americans may have been on their way to the United States and Canada accompanying Mexicans from southern states such as Chiapas and Veracruz who were beginning to migrate as well. However, other data suggests that a portion of these refugees may have stayed in Mexico, although no one knows how many. Surveys of undocumented Central Americans who arrived in the United States suggest that many share similar backgrounds with their Mexican counterparts, in that they come from rural areas and have less than high school educations.[22] As long as Mexican migration to the north remains at current levels, this could mean a direct competition for low-skilled jobs amongst Mexican and Central American immigrants.

Mexico has always been a destination for immigrants who, like nearly a million U.S. citizens, want to live or retire there. However, its territory has also become a pass-through for third-nationals seeking entry to the United States, some from as far away as Asia, Africa, and the Middle East. Still, by most accounts, Central Americans comprise the largest group of migrants entering and transiting Mexican territory.

With employment prospects currently improving in Mexico, some of these migrants may decide to stay. On Mexico's southern boundary, there is a history of cross-border commerce and legal seasonal visitation for agricultural work in Mexican states like Chiapas, Oaxaca, and Veracruz—and during the conflicts of the 1980s, Guatemalans and Salvadorans sought refuge in Mexico. Following peace agreements in Central America, regular migratory movements resumed as more Central Americans left war-ravaged economies to seek work in the north (Figure 6).

Although economic growth has been robust in Central America's northern triangle states of El Salvador, Guatemala, and Honduras, their demographic characteristics resemble those in Mexico that, two decades ago, promoted outward flows. Guatemala and Honduras still have robust population growth rates and youth bulges.[23] The average years of schooling

22. Brick et al., *Mexican and Central American Immigrants in the United States*, pp. 7–8.
23. National socio-demographic profiles at CEPALSTAT, Databases and Statistical Publications, Economic Commission for Latin America and the Caribbean (ECLAC), United Nations, http://estadisticas.cepal.org/cepalstat/WEB_CEPALSTAT/perfilesNacionales.asp?idioma=i.

Central American migrants board a freight train outside Tenosique, Tabasco near the Mexico-Guatemala border to ride what they call *La Bestia (*the beast) north in search of work. Photo: Migration in Tenosique; Credit: Marilyn Alvarado Leyva, Repositorio Península, Creative Commons, FLICKR at http://www.flickr.com/photos/78592498@N02/7284704006/sizes/l/in/photostream.

in the three nations are extremely low.[24] Current statistics show poverty rates in El Salvador and Guatemala above 45 percent, while they are more than 65 percent in Honduras. As of 2010, 21 percent of the workforce was employed in the agriculture sector in El Salvador; some 31 percent works in that capacity in Guatemala, and 36 percent of workers toil in the agriculture in Honduras.[25] By comparison, only about 13 percent of the labor force now works in agriculture in Mexico.

Economic growth is more varied for the northern triangle states, but growth rates for all three appear to have slowed over the past four years.[26] Meanwhile, educational attainment, poverty rates (Figure 7), and sectorial employment statistics all suggest that upward economic growth has not yet resulted in sufficient progress for these nations' poor. This situation has led to crime waves that make the three northern triangle states some of the most violent places in the world. In 2011, the homicide rate in Honduras was 91.6 per 100,000 people—the highest in the world.[27] Most assaults, murders, and robberies occur in poor urban areas where rural youth come seeking work.

On one hand, as mentioned above, fewer Mexicans are likely to migrate north—though this change may come slowly—in the coming years. On the other hand, security threats and unemployment in these three Central American countries raise the likelihood of their populations' migrating. Given the similarities between Mexican and other Central American

24. Robert Barro and Jong-Wha Lee, "Educational Attainment for Population Aged 15 and Over," Barro-Lee Educational Attainment Dataset, 2010, http://www.barrolee.com.

25. National socio-demographic profiles at CEPALSTAT, http://estadisticas.cepal.org/cepalstat/WEB_CEPALSTAT/perfilesNacionales.asp?idioma=i.

26. World Bank, "World DataBank: World Development Indicators," http://databank.worldbank.org/ddp/editReport?REQUEST_SOURCE=search&CNO=2&country=HND&series=&period=.

27. "Intentional homicide, count and rate per 100,000 population (1995–2011)," UNODC Homicide Statistics, United Nations Office on Drugs and Crime, http://www.unodc.org/unodc/en/data-and-analysis/homicide.html.

Figure 6. Central American Migrant Flows in Mexico (thousands)

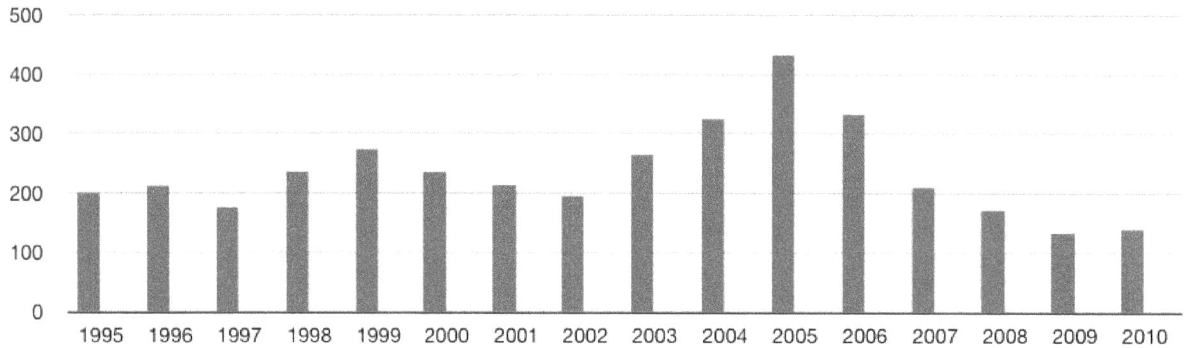

From statistics on Central American migrants detained in Mexico, on the U.S. border, and estimates of those who entered the United States. Source: Gustavo Mohar, "U.S.-Mexico Migration – The New Landscape," presentation at Center for Strategic and International Studies, Washington, DC, February 9, 2013, http://csis.org/event/us-mexico-migration-new-landscape.

immigrants looking for jobs in the United States, workers from the northern triangle states will be motivated to replace the ones that once came from Mexico. That said, the demand for labor in the United States remains pivotal in driving migrant flows. As such, Central American immigrants will replace Mexicans only as long as the demand for manual labor in the United States remains high enough to drive illegal entry.

Mexican authorities are well aware of the complicated social and economic situation of these Central American countries. In fact, Mexico has shown increasing willingness to help Central American neighbors.

In 1996, it hosted the first of many meetings of the Regional Conference on Migration—a vice-ministerial forum that discusses humanitarian and security aspects of Central and North American movements.[28] In 1998, it consolidated various foreign aid efforts under its new Institute for International Cooperation to improve outreach to Central American neighbors. Arriving in office in 2000, President Vicente Fox promised a development initiative called *Plan Puebla-Panamá*, intended to help Central America, as well as Mexico, build a foundation for greater prosperity through large infrastructure projects. And in 2004, Mexico joined the Central American Integration System (SICA) as an observer to coordinate on regional security issues.

Still, much of the difficulty experienced by El Salvador, Guatemala, and Honduras that would impact migrant flows have to do with improving the quality of political leadership, growing institutional capacity, modernizing and streamlining regulatory frameworks, and changing old antipathies toward rule of law that would help boost economic activity and, in turn, job growth at home. These are generational projects that will primarily require sustained local commitment. Still, partnerships will be needed from North American neighbors, as well as other countries in Latin America that have developed free-market economies and established accountable, democratic political systems. Moreover, as Mexican migration to its

28. Members include: Belize, Canada, Costa Rica, the Dominican Republic, El Salvador, Guatemala, Honduras, Mexico, Nicaragua, Panama, and the United States. See Regional Conference on Migration, "General Information," http://www.rcmvs.org/Descripcion.htm.

Figure 7. Northern Triangle Poverty Rates (percent of population)

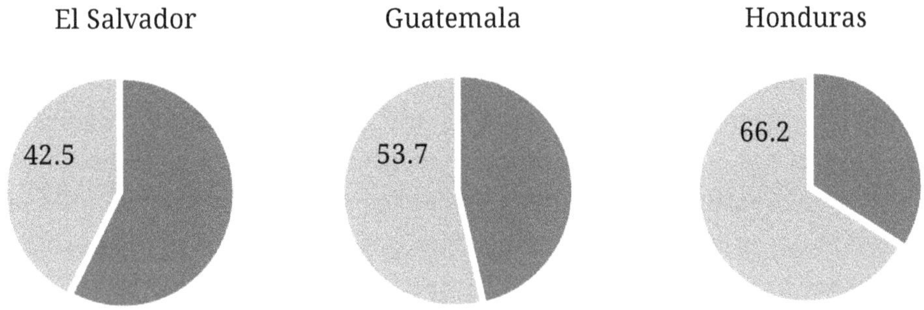

Source: Data, The World Bank at http://data.worldbank.org.

northern neighbor fades and Mexico becomes more of a labor partner of the United States, the two can work together to tackle Central American issues in a joint effort.

Conclusion

In closing, it is imperative that we realize three things:

- First, the drivers of migration are well understood. Little incentivizes migration more than a lack of opportunities at home, their availability abroad, and access to the information about and means to take advantage of those opportunities.
- Second, after a long history of Mexican-dominated southern immigration to the United States, a gradual effort to reform Mexico's economy portends a sea change in the country's excess supply of labor—and thus of the demographic makeup of the immigrants entering the United States. And as Mexicans play a decreasing role in migratory patterns, they will likely be replaced by their Central American neighbors, who themselves face domestic conditions not dissimilar to Mexico's in recent decades.
- Finally, as these patterns shift, it is in both Mexico's and the United States' interest to work together with Central American countries to address those challenges Mexico is beginning to overcome, but are now borne by its Central American counterparts.[29]

Though it may not have always been apparent, Mexico has been on a trajectory to reduce inequality and create a modern democracy since the Mexican Revolution in 1910. Along the way, some ventures such as land tenure and the creation of state-run business proved misguided, while others, like import substitution strategies to jump-start native industries, were employed beyond their usefulness.

Vestiges of colonial rule in the form of corruption, clientelistic practices, and impunity impeded the formation of a government by the people and for the people at all levels. Mexico's democratic constitution limits elected officials from seeking consecutive terms to ward off dictatorship, yet the country had single-party rule from the 1930s until 2000—which itself

29. See below for a full set of recommendations for the United States and Mexico moving forward.

contributed to the formation of an entrenched class of political insiders, kept local government weak, and depressed feelings of national ownership on the part of many citizens.

To the extent that current trends in Mexican economics and politics can be extended—to further open the economy, develop human capital, and ensure that more citizens have a personal stake in their country—pressures driving migration based on an exhaustion of domestic opportunities will decrease. What has historically seemed to be an intractable problem between the United States and Mexico is, for the first time, showing signs of easing—and may well continue to recede as we move forward.

Nevertheless challenges remain. Upwards of one-third of Mexicans live below the poverty line, and many continue to see few available opportunities at home. While Mexico is a resource-rich country well able to mitigate these problems on its own, the United States can provide assistance by quietly affirming successful reforms and encouraging the Peña Nieto government to carry out its promises to boost competitiveness, curb corruption, improve education, and further rural development. Moreover, the United States would be well served by continuing to provide material support for more effective governance at the state and local levels and by aiding Mexico's efforts to strengthen law enforcement and the judicial system—all of which benefit Mexican and U.S. security.

Still of concern are residual migrant flows through Mexico on the part of Central Americans, as many try to escape criminal violence, poverty, and poor job prospects still farther south—and, to some extent, in countries beyond North American shores. Key to dealing with the inevitably changing demographics of migrant groups is helping countries of origin confront the root problems that incentivize their citizens to leave. To the degree that long-term support for Mexican political and economic reforms has helped to alter the incentives migrants face, similar actions on the part of the United States and Mexico can help affect prosperity and alleviate migratory pressures in Central America.

Efforts toward comprehensive immigration reform would create an important, reliable legal framework for immigration flows. The bill currently being debated in the Senate has three core provisions: the extension of legal status to undocumented immigrants—and an eventual path to U.S. citizenship; the strengthening of border security; and bolstered work programs to facilitate the entry and hiring of both high- and low-skilled foreign workers. Each of these three carries distinct implications for the future of immigration to the United States.

By extending legal status to the 11 million undocumented migrants already living within U.S. borders, the bill would send a clear message to those migrants—the vast majority of whom have actively participated in the labor force and paid taxes despite their illegal status—that their contributions to the country are valued. And, from a more hard-headed perspective, doing so would enable them to participate more thoroughly in the economic and political life of the country, providing invaluable contributions to both. There are those that raise concerns that extending legal status to undocumented migrants only encourages more illegal immigration in the future, implying future rounds of amnesty as well. While this concern may well be legitimate, the bill currently being considered brings with it improvements in border security meant to counteract that effect. By further securing the southwest border, the new legislation renders largely moot many of the concerns that amnesty would encourage immigration down the line.

Finally, the bill's plan to bolster work programs for both high- and low-skilled foreign workers is pivotal to immigration patterns. As discussed above, the Bracero Program of the 1940s was uniquely successful in that it encouraged the circular flow of migrant labor—rather than permanent immigration. By providing seasonal or temporary jobs to workers at times of peak U.S. demand for labor, the program was able to meet that demand without substantially increasing the population of permanent migrant residents in the United States.

Recommendations

From conflict to lack of economic opportunity, the conditions that drive migrant flows are costly. Origin countries lose talent and productive potential. Destination countries, while benefiting from legal flows, are burdened with unauthorized entrants ill-prepared to live in unfamiliar circumstances.

As history shows, identifying solutions is not easy. The sense of urgency often falls on the destination country—hence U.S. insistence on easing migratory flows through improved border security. In recent years, senior U.S. leaders have pursued a subtler track, encouraging their Mexican counterparts in their efforts to strengthen economic performance at home. Over time, these efforts have resulted in a strategic trade agreement, supported more careful management of the Mexican economy, and affirmed Mexican efforts to carry out further reforms.

Looking forward, the United States should continue support for measures that will make Mexico more competitive and reduce economic imbalances.

For its part, Mexico should continue to press forward to exploit its creative potential and, at the same time, strengthen domestic rule of law to encourage foreign investment. Both countries should take advantage of the current lull in migratory pressure to adopt policies that channel migrants into safe, legal pathways. Finally, both should cooperate in supporting security, governance, and economic reforms in Central America as migrants from El Salvador, Guatemala, and Honduras still cross borders to seek safety and jobs in Mexico or the United States.

FOR THE UNITED STATES

Patient, long-term encouragement for political and economic reforms has proven the most effective means of reducing unauthorized migration movements. The smaller the economic disparities between source and destination countries, the less pressure there is on the population to migrate.

Senior officials in the George H.W. Bush and Carlos Salinas administrations were aware of this when they established a working relationship that culminated in NAFTA.[30] Thanks to the cooperative spirit on both sides, momentum continued for an ongoing series of economic and electoral reforms.

30. González, *Dual Transitions from Authoritarian Rule*, pp. 192–3.

The objective now should be to keep that momentum going. Even though Mexico remains nationalist and proud toward its northern neighbor, it is more willing to accept advice and assistance from the United States than ever before—something propelled by Calderón's administration and continued by Peña Nieto thus far. Contrary to Mexico's standpoint, given that Mexico is doing well economically and that it is becoming a leader in the international community, the U.S. Congress has become reticent about providing assistance. Both legislative and executive branches in the United States should be encouraged to continue supporting Mexico. Given these conditions, the United States should:

- Discretely encourage ongoing reform efforts and share information that would make Mexico's economy more competitive, focusing on ways to strengthen property rights, improve local governance, and bolster education, all of which could further open economic and job opportunities.
- Continue security cooperation under the Mérida Initiative, especially in the administration of justice to make law enforcement more effective and to strengthen governance at the local level where it is weakest. As criminal system reforms near completion, the United States should offer to share its experience on civil procedures and improving the commercial code.
- Deepen its partnership with Mexico and multilateral financial institutions to promote better border security, governance, and economic reforms in Central America in an effort to ease the pressures that drive the region's citizens to migrate.

FOR MEXICO

Thanks to more effective fiscal and monetary management, as well as an expanding network of free-trade agreements (Mexico is now part of 12 such agreements with 44 countries), Mexico ended its late-twentieth century of financial crises, sustained modest economic growth since the late 1990s, emerged from the 2009 global recession still plaguing its biggest trade partner, the United States, and for two years has posted a growth rate exceeding that of Brazil. However, more change is needed to develop the kind of broad prosperity that will keep significant numbers of workers from migrating to escape still-high rural poverty levels. Mexican policymakers should consider:

- Further expanding trade relationships. Mexico should strive to better connect itself with Pacific and Asian markets through the Trans-Pacific Partnership (TPP). Aside from Japan, Mexico does not currently have any far-reaching free-trade agreements with Asia. An institutionalized agreement like the TPP will diversify Mexico's export and import sources while strengthening foreign direct investment (FDI) from nations aside from the United States. Likewise, Mexico should push for its inclusion in the Transatlantic Trade and Investment Partnership (TTIP) between the United States and the European Union. The EU-U.S. trade relationship is the largest in the world,[31] and although Mexico already benefits from low tariffs and strong FDI stemming from a trade agree-

31. European Commission, "Transatlantic Trade and Investment Partnership (TTIP)," June 2013, http://ec.europa.eu/trade/policy/in-focus/ttip/.

ment with the EU, having access to a €2 billion market with minimal regulations would boost Mexico's economy and global competitiveness.

- Reforming the currently uncompetitive oil industry. Lawmakers should push for changes to allow foreign investment in Pemex, the state-owned oil company, to create a public-foreign partnership, and to detach it from serving as a direct source of revenue for the federal budget. A more productive and globally competitive oil industry would not only bolster Mexico's development, but also have substantial spillover effects in innovation and employment. President Peña Nieto should be encouraged to move forward with the oil industry reforms proposed in his *Pacto por México* in December 2012.
- Improving local governance and rule of law. In 2011, Mexico ranked in the 25th percentile in political stability, and between the 25th and 50th percentile in both rule of law and corruption.[32] This lack of good governance undermines not only democracy and social justice, but also the market economy. Foreign investors are and will continue to be reluctant to enter rural zones—even those with abundant natural resources—when facing corruption and lackluster protection of property rights. Preventing economic activity to flourish in these areas will then hinder their development, and unemployment as well as poverty will persist. To improve the situation, the federal government should support the state and local governments providing what is necessary for the latter to raise more of their own revenue and to implement and enforce existing laws. Trust in the justice system will improve citizen security and promote a better business climate.

32. The percentile indicates Mexico's ranking among all countries in the world. World Bank, "World Governance Indicators," http://info.worldbank.org/governance/wgi/sc_chart.asp.

Resources

CONFERENCES

"Dealing with the Causes: Mexico's Economic Policy and Migration." Washington, D.C.: Americas Program, Center for Strategic and International Studies, January 2011.

"Mexico: Elections and Prospects for Structural Reform." Washington, D.C.: Americas Program, Center for Strategic and International Studies, May 2012.

"U.S.-Mexico Migration: The New Landscape." Washington, D.C.: Americas Program, Center for Strategic and International Studies, February 2013.

REPORTS

Graybeal, Michael. "Mexico's Economic Policy and Migration: Dealing with the Causes." Washington, D.C.: Americas Program, Center for Strategic and International Studies, May 2011

Graybeal, Michael. "U.S.-Mexico Migration–Prospects for Reform." Washington, D.C.: Americas Program, Center for Strategic and International Studies, January 2012.

Johnson, Stephen. "Could July 1 Elections Impact Mexico's Progress?" Washington, D.C.: Americas Program, Center for strategic and International Studies, May 2012.

Johnson, Stephen, and Alek Suni. "Mexican Labor Reforms–What Do They Mean?" Washington, D.C.: Americas Program, Center for Strategic and International Studies, December 2012.

BLOG POSTS

Sánchez Zinny, Gabriel. "Mexico must focus on human capital to achieve its full potential." Americas Program Blog. Washington, D.C.: Center for Strategic and International Studies, December 2012.

About the Authors

Carl Meacham is director of the CSIS Americas Program. He joined CSIS from the Senate Foreign Relations Committee (SFRC), where he served on the professional staff for Senator Richard Lugar (R-IN) for over a decade. He served as the senior adviser for Latin America and the Caribbean on the committee, the most senior Republican Senate staff position for this region. In that capacity, he traveled extensively to the region to work with foreign governments, private-sector organizations, and civil society groups. He was also responsible for managing the committee's relationship with the State Department regarding the Western Hemisphere and overseeing its $2 billion budget.

Before he joined SFRC, Meacham worked on the staff of two Democratic senators. Prior to his Senate work, he served at the Department of Commerce as special assistant to the deputy secretary, at the Cuban Affairs Bureau of the Department of State, and at the U.S. embassy in Madrid. Meacham is a native speaker of Spanish and was partly raised in Chile, his mother's country of origin. He received his B.A. from the University at Albany, State University of New York, and holds M.A. degrees from American University and Columbia University.

Michael Graybeal is the program coordinator for the Americas Program and previously served as the research associate to the William E. Simon Chair in Political Economy. He joined CSIS in May 2010 after receiving his M.A. in Latin American studies from Georgetown University. While completing his master's degree, he spent time in Chile conducting research on the U.S.-Chile Free Trade Agreement. He holds a B.A. in history from the University of Pittsburgh and is fluent in Spanish.

www.ingramcontent.com/pod-product-compliance
Ingram Content Group UK Ltd.
Pitfield, Milton Keynes, MK11 3LW, UK
UKHW051418150926
475561UK00005B/235

9 781442 224957